This book is dedicated to every person who has at some point seen themselves as less than GREAT!
You spend more time with you than anyone else...
Stay on your team! Chase your dreams! Consistently work on being the very best version of yourself that you can be!
After all, there is a little Fred and Mary in all of us!

For bulk orders, speaking engagements, or school presentations, contact us at info@lkobiedawiz.com.

ISBN: 978-09-979667-9-4-7

Library of Congress Control Number: 2007905210

Graphic Design by Aaron J. Ratzlaff and L. Kobie Wilkerson III.

Second Edition

Please visit us at the official website:
WWW.LKOBIEDAWIZ.COM

FRED AND MARY

L. KOBIE DA WIZ

illustrated by AARON J. RATZLAFF

LOVE II LEARN BOOKS

ATLANTA

This is a funny story about a couple,

but the message is important,

so listen carefully to what is said.

Once upon a time
there was a guy named Fred.
And Fred had hair on his head,
and it was red.

Now, Fred loved the hair on his head,

and not simply because it was red.

It was short and curly and of good health,

but Fred, outside the hair on his head,

wasn't concerned about too much else.

All Fred knew about

was his hair.

Other aspects of hygiene,

I don't think he too much cared.

His teeth were black,

and his breath, it smelled.

And we won't discuss

his skin and his nails.

But despite all of this,
    Fred was happy anyway.
    He went about his business,
    not caring what people had to say.
They talked about his clothes
    and his beat-up shoes,
    but none of these things
    gave Fred the blues.

Whatever they'd say,

he would always reply,

"Can't talk about my hair?"

and wink his eye.

Then he'd continue
on his merry way,
still not caring
what people had to say.

One day while walking,

Fred met this girl named Mary.

She was quite cute,

but a tad bit hairy.

She had hairy arms
and hairy legs,
and boy, did she ever have
hair on her head.
She walked up to Fred,
and to Fred she said,

"I really like the hair on your head!"

Fred was so shocked
  that she had recognized
  that big fat tears
  almost came to his eyes.
But being strong,
  he held them back,
  and as he reached up
  to his hair to pat,
He said, "Why, ma'am,
  you truly are so kind.
  You have such nice hair,
  yet you compliment mine."
She said, "Oh, it's nothing.
  Your hair is truly nice.
  Trust me, I know lots about hair.
  I've had lots all my life."

Now I did tell you that Mary was cute,

but I didn't tell you about

how big her feet were

and how she smelled like puke!

But Fred didn't mind

any of that.

She liked his hair,

and that was that.

Now Fred and Mary fell in love
and went off and got married,
and I can tell you that the sight
was truly kind of scary.
But married life
did them both some good.
It got them to a place
that it should.
Because of marriage,
their lives improved . . .

Mary took baths and got some new shoes.

Fred got some new clothes

and some new kicks,

and believe it or not . . .

he got his teeth fixed.

His skin and his nails

were the picture of perfect health,

and Fred and Mary were happy

without anyone else.

They lived on happily
and had a few kids,
because plenty of joy and love
they had to give.
It just goes to show:
regardless of what you look like outside,
it's what you've got inside
that makes you survive.

There are Freds and Marys
all over the world.
They are men and women,
boys and girls.

See, Fred and Mary understood
this one thing
more than anyone else,
and that is . . .

before you go

and love someone else,

you must first love yourself.

I LOVE ME

I look in the mirror and what do I see?
I see someone who really likes me!
I work real hard, and keep my behavior royal.
I treat others kind and to myself I'll be loyal!
I'm smart and beautiful and have nice words to say,
and there is no one like me and I love this face!
I'm so special because there is no one just like me!
I look in the mirror and you know what I see?
I see someone who loves themself,
and if they could be anyone in the world
they'd be no one else!
You give me a chance to be anyone I could be,
and every single time I'd choose me!
I look in the mirror and I'm impressed!
I see someone who always does their best!
No matter what may happen, or what may be,
I will always remember how I feel about me!

I LOVE ME! I LOVE ME! I LOVE ME!

I LOVE ME BECAUSE ...

_____

_____

_____

_____

_____

_____

_____

_____

_____

_____

_____

_____

I LOVE ME! I LOVE ME! I LOVE ME!